A story to help with...

WORRY THOUGHTS

Corbett Shwom

Note to Parents and Caregivers

At the end of the book, you'll find two coloring pages that can be used as an activity to complement the book. They are of the same page, just one has the symbolic worry thoughts and the other does not. I thought it would be a wonderful idea to allow the reader or listener to write in their own worries with the messaging that the page provides. You can also download these coloring pages from the Worry Thoughts site under 'Resources'.

Published by Worry House Press.
First Edition
Printed in the United States of America.

www.worrythoughts.com

To Emma and Abby

Dear Reader,

Worry thoughts can sneak up on anyone, big or small. They might make you feel worried or scared, but remember, everyone has worries sometimes, and you're not alone.

Inside, you'll find a special poem that I wrote for my daughters when they were young to help them deal with their worries. It helped them a lot, especially at bedtime. You'll learn that worries are just thoughts and nothing more, and you don't have to let them take over.

Also included in the book is a comic strip of the poem, as well as the original poem, with the hope that the book can always be your go-to as you grow up.

Remember, it's okay to feel worried sometimes, just don't give the worries too much attention.

So, let's take a deep breath and together explore how to take control of those worry thoughts.

Warm hugs,
Emma and Abby's Dad

Storybook

Lots of thoughts everyday

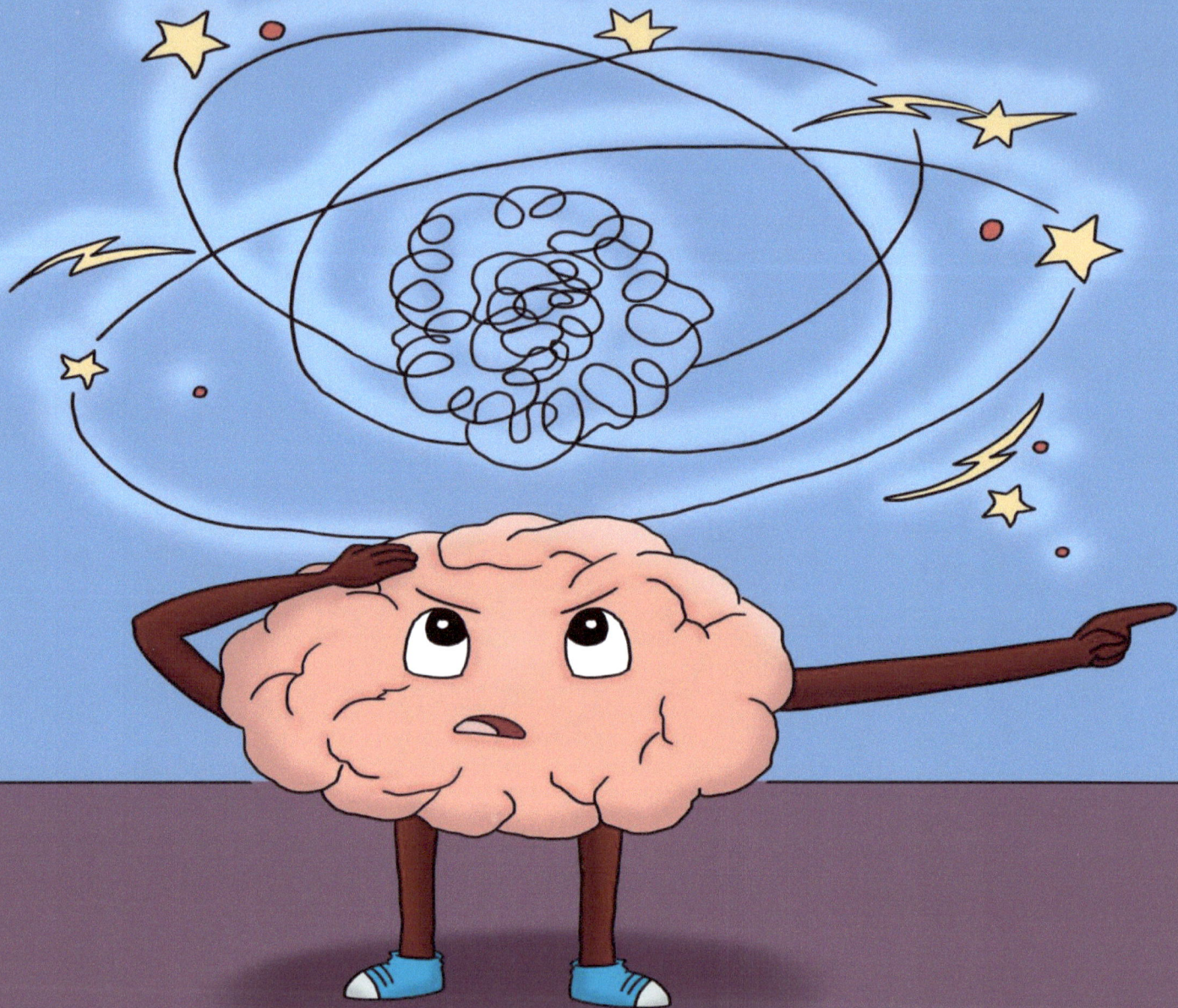

Some of them just don't go away

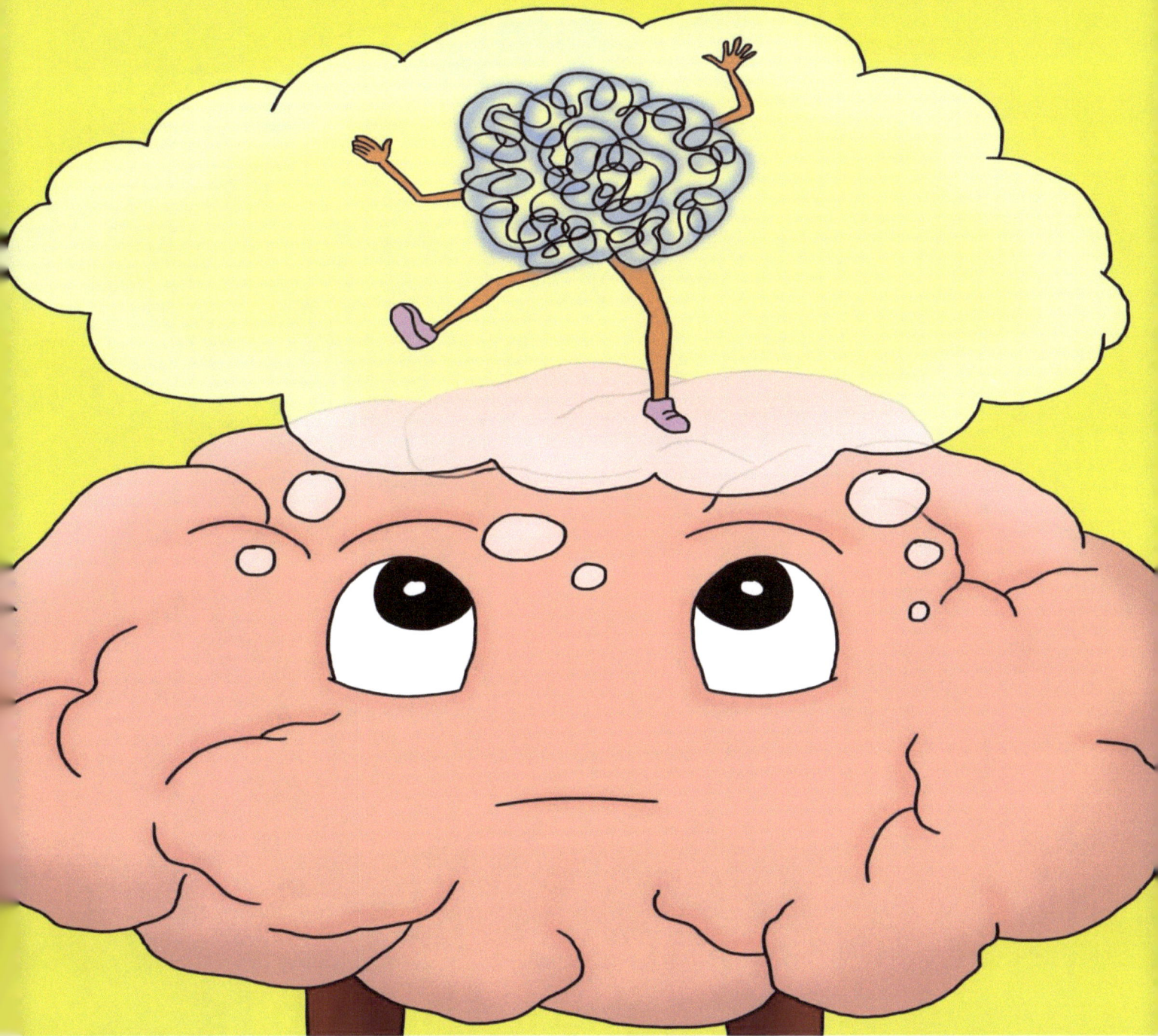

Dancing around on your mind's floor

They are just thoughts
and nothing more

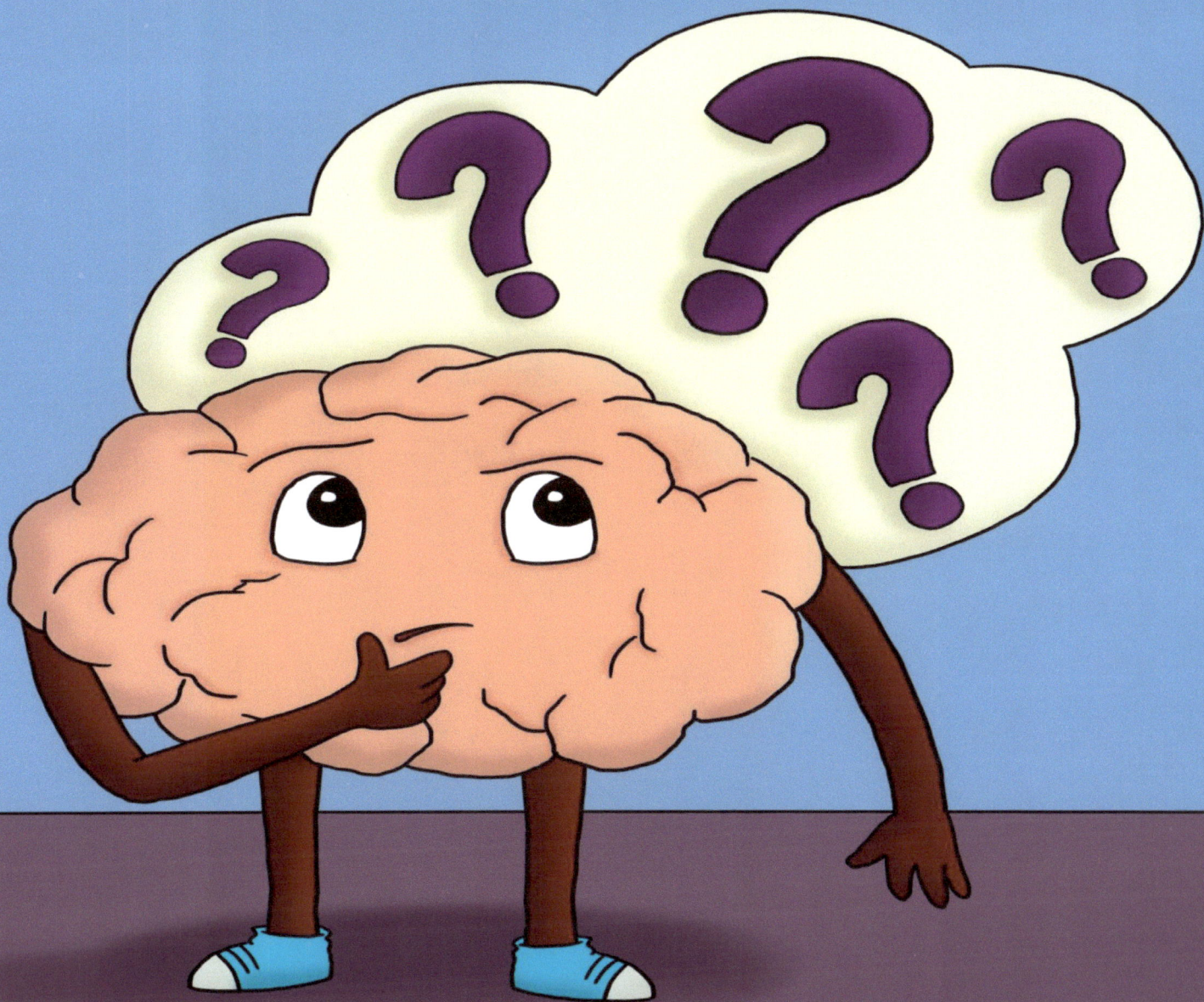

You wonder why you think them
and when they will go away

No one knows for sure
or how long it is they will stay

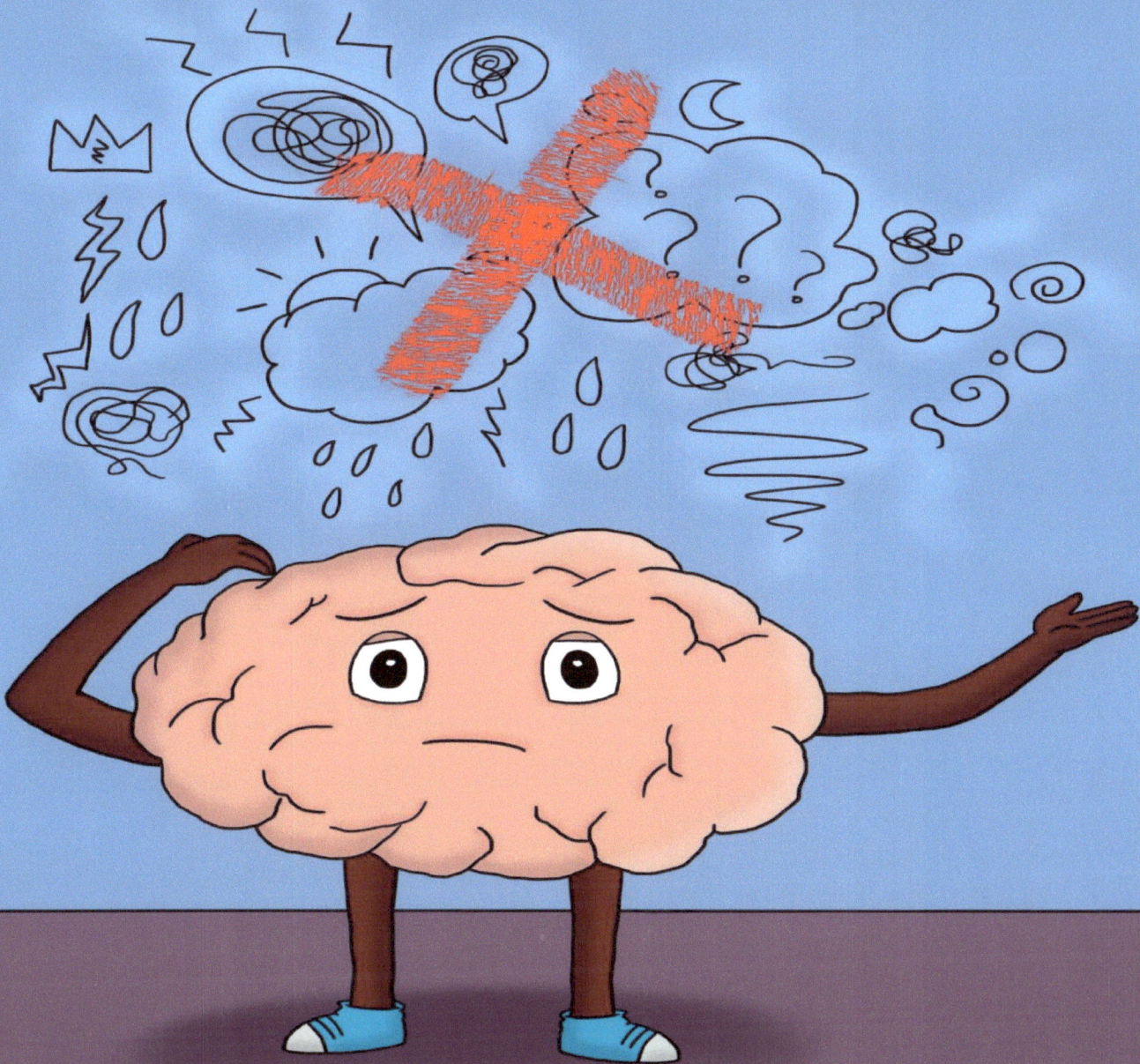

But just because you think them, doesn't make them true

Your mind isn't magic,
so don't let them upset you

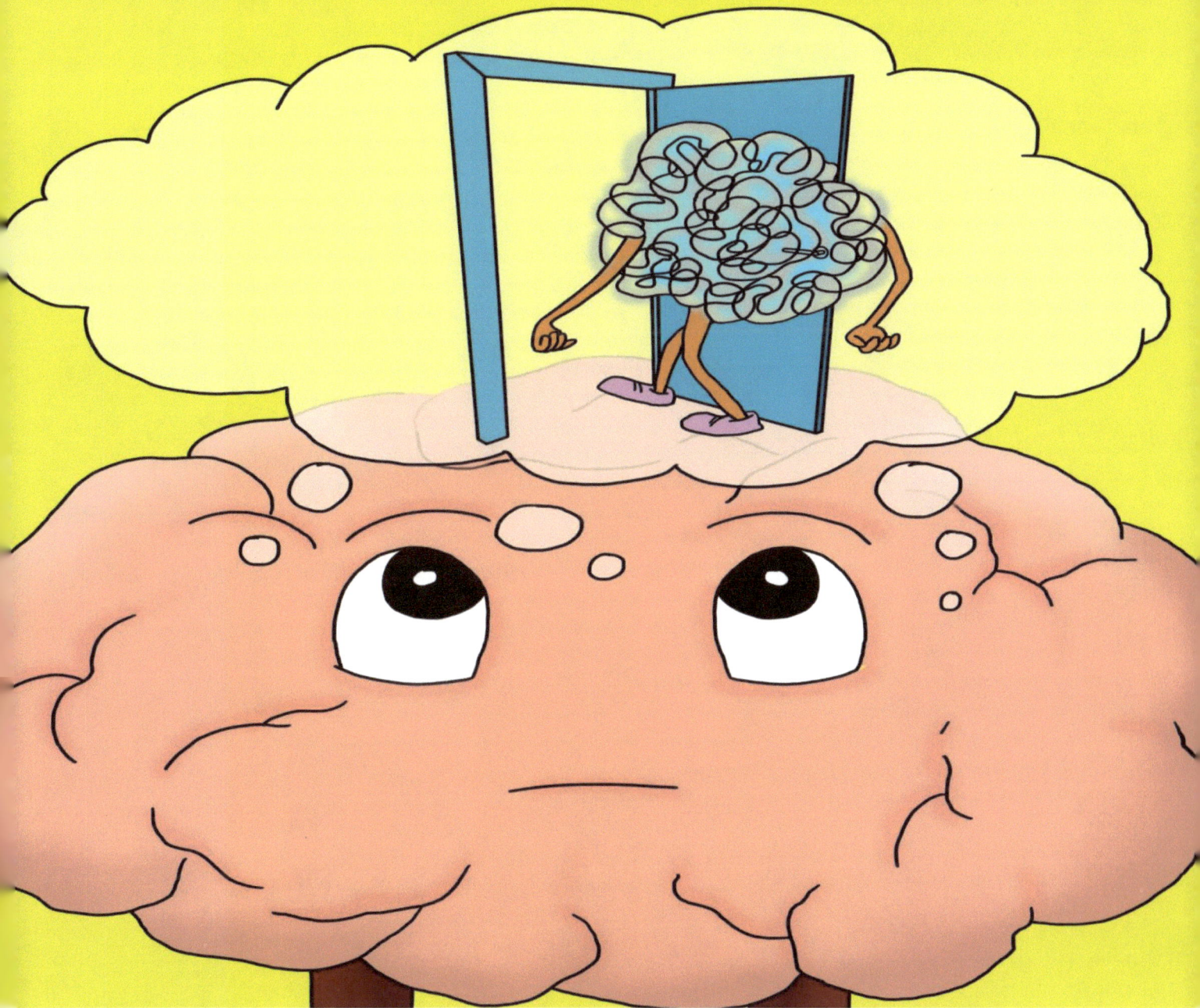

They are in and out of your mind's door

Still they are just thoughts
and nothing more

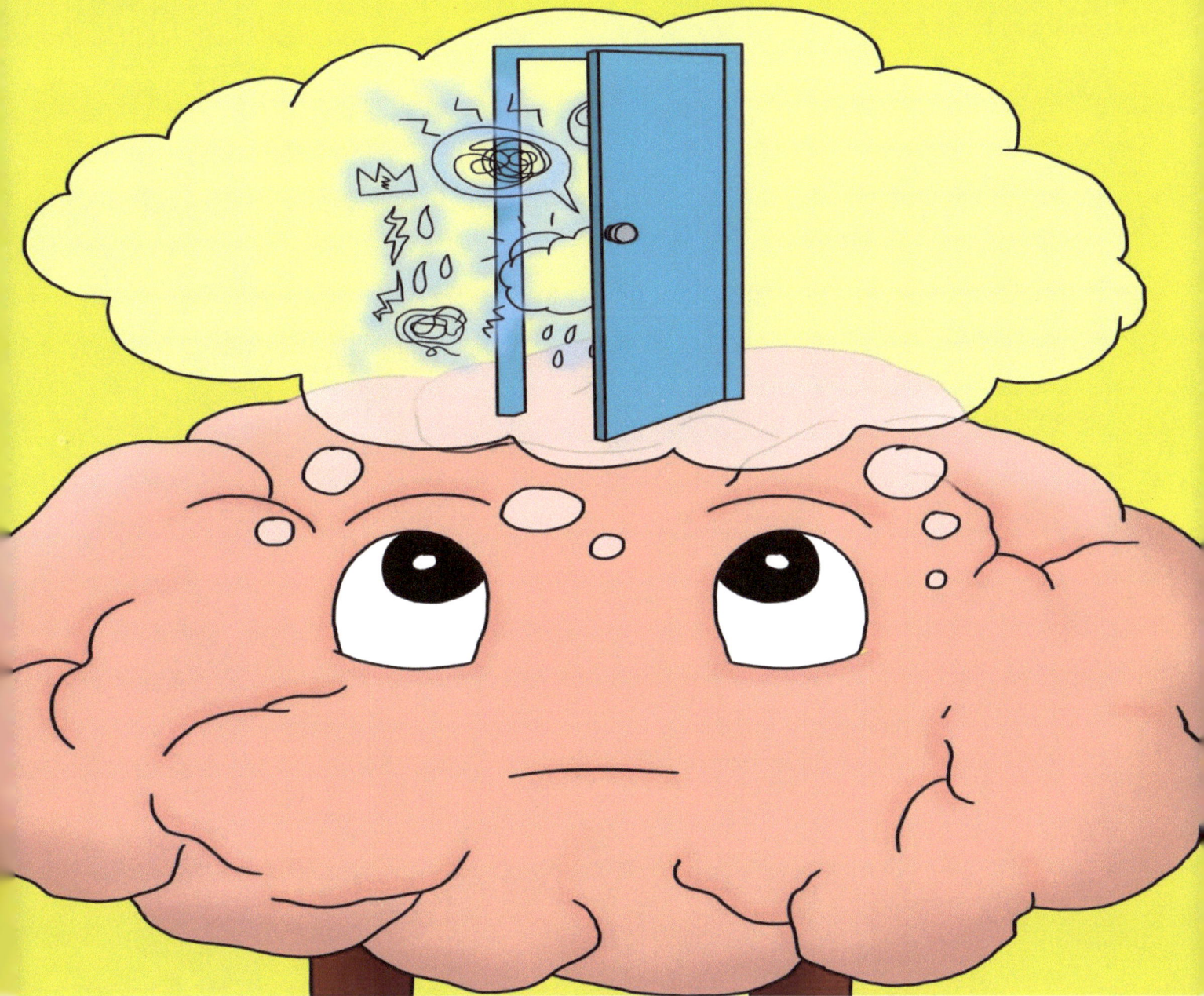

Are they still there
you check to see

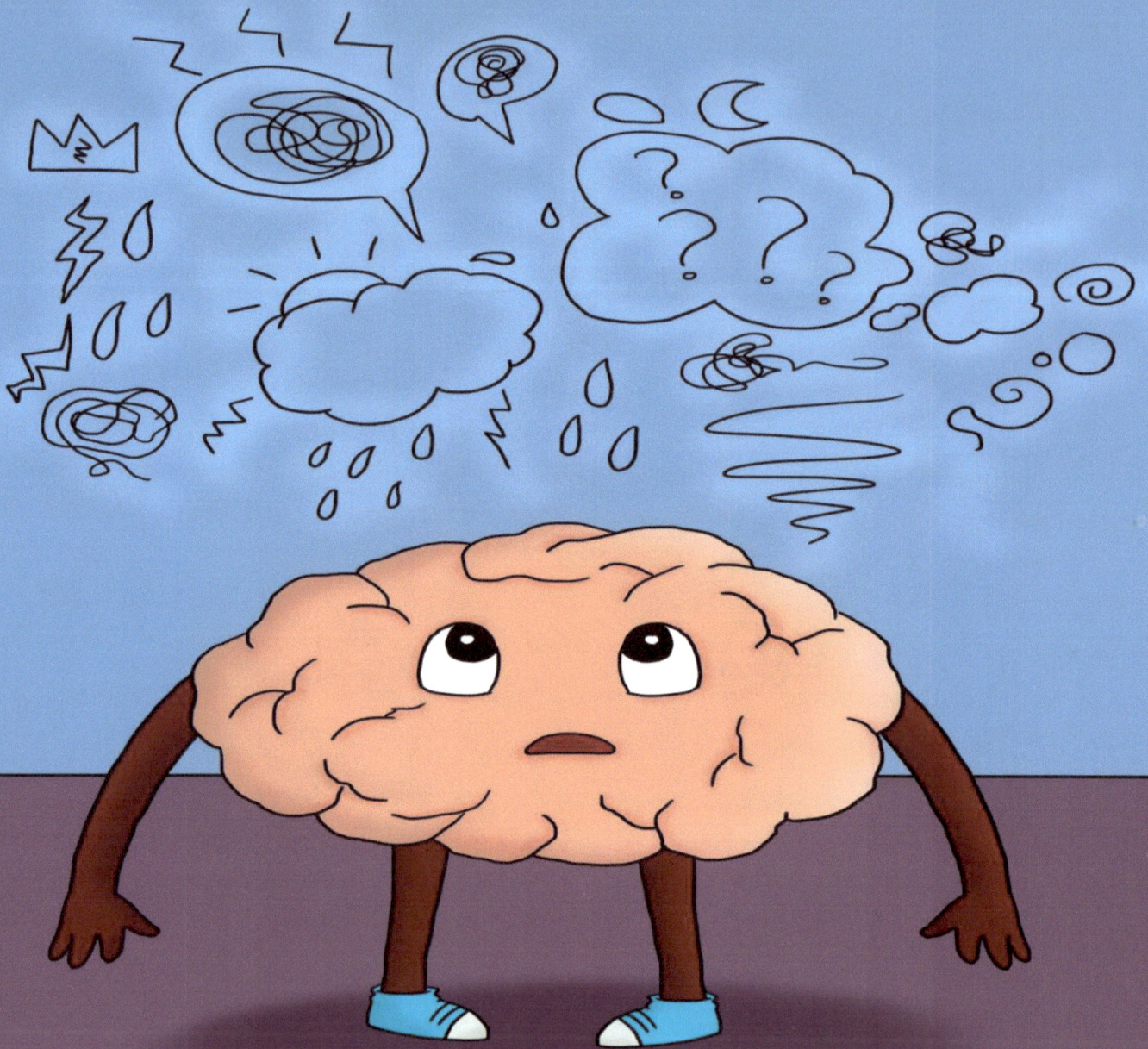

But by doing such
you make them be

Simply let them come and go

For without any attention
there is no show

But for the ones that are
still your mind's chore

Remember, they are just thoughts and nothing more

Comic Strip

Lots of thoughts everyday

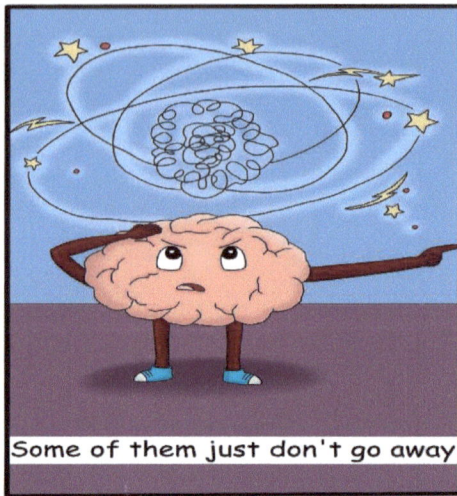
Some of them just don't go away

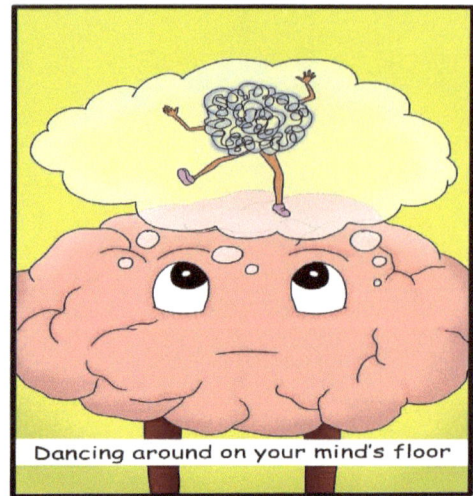
Dancing around on your mind's floor

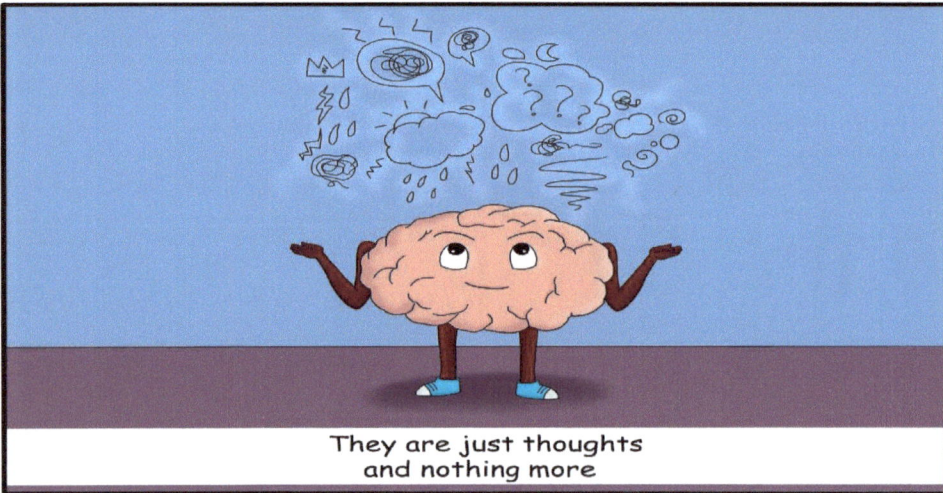
They are just thoughts
and nothing more

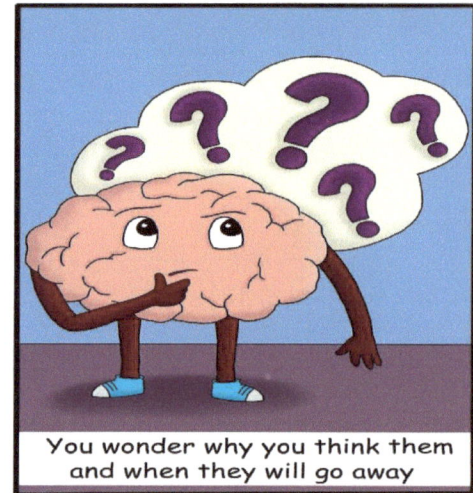
You wonder why you think them
and when they will go away

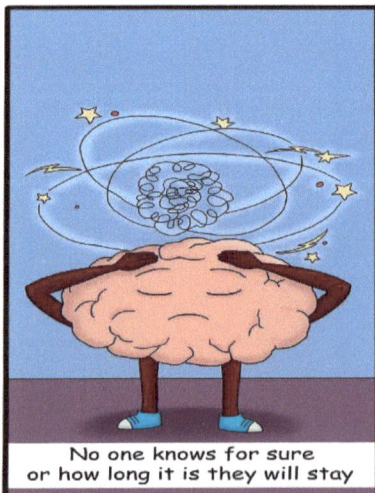
No one knows for sure
or how long it is they will stay

But just because you think them,
doesn't make them true

Your mind isn't magic,
so don't let them upset you

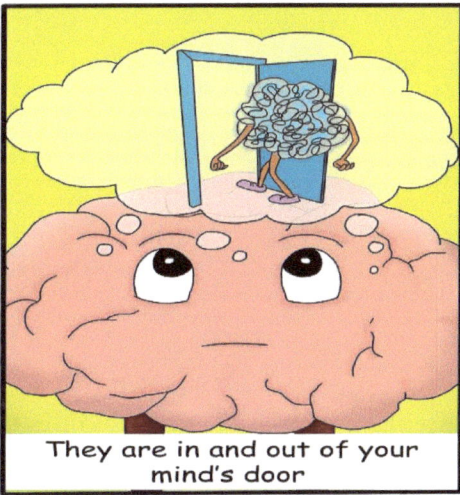

They are in and out of your mind's door

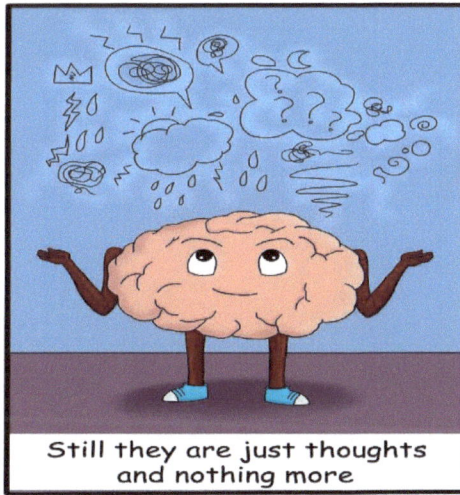

Still they are just thoughts and nothing more

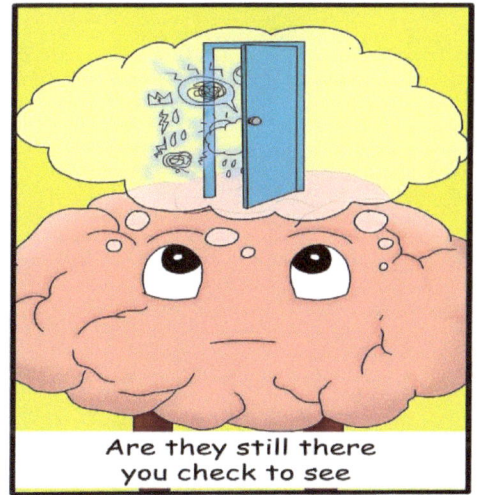

Are they still there you check to see

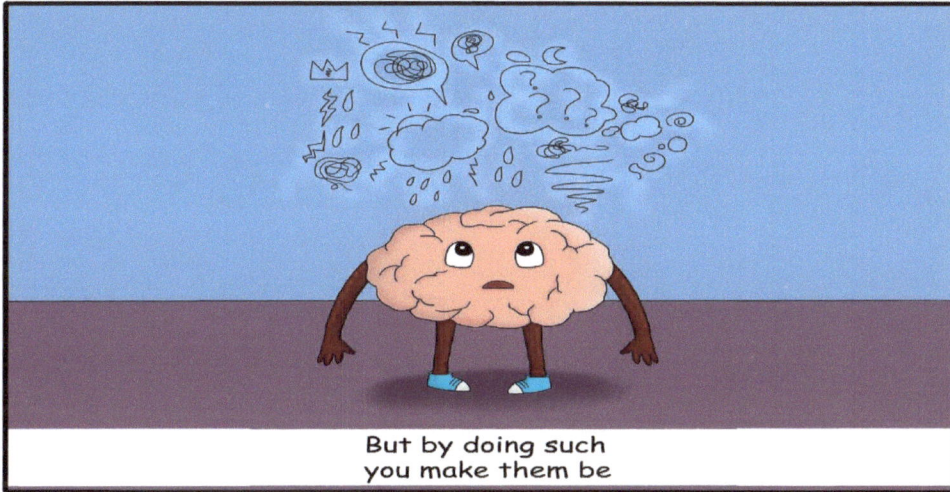

But by doing such you make them be

Simply let them come and go

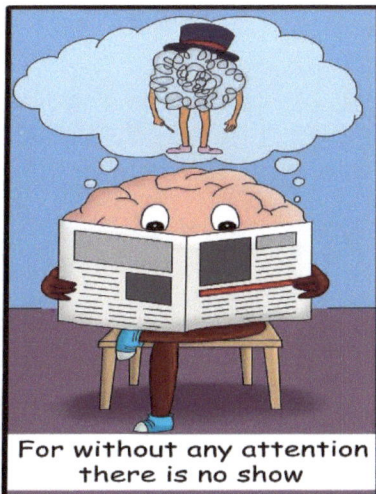

For without any attention there is no show

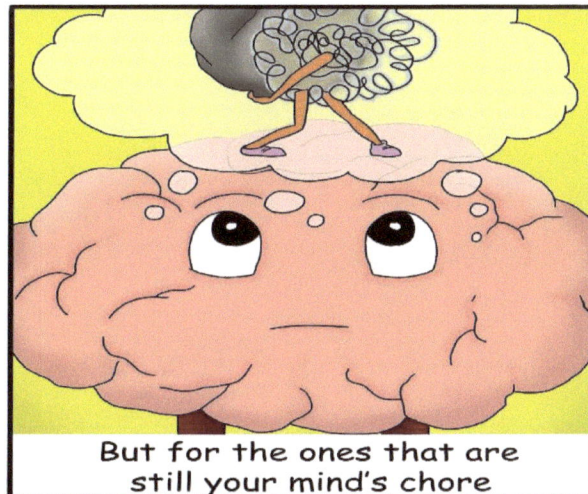

But for the ones that are still your mind's chore

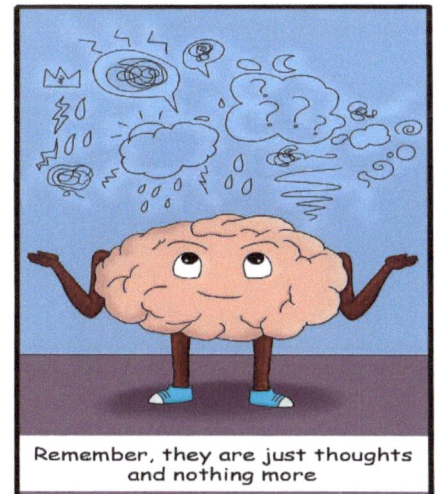

Remember, they are just thoughts and nothing more

Poem

Lots of thoughts everyday
Some of them just don't go away
Dancing around on your mind's floor
They are just thoughts and nothing more
You wonder why you think them and when they will go away
No one knows for sure or how long it is they will stay
But just because you think them, doesn't make them true
Your mind isn't magic, so don't let them upset you
They are in and out of your mind's door
Still they are just thoughts and nothing more
Are they still there you check to see
But by doing such you make them be
Simply let them come and go
For without any attention there is no show
But for the ones that are still your mind's chore
Remember, they are just thoughts and nothing more

They are just thoughts
and nothing more

They are just thoughts
and nothing more

Other Titles By Corbett Shwom

Worry Habits
A Story to Help Children Better Understand and Manage OCD

Worry Shy
A Story to Help Children Better Understand and Manage Social Anxiety

Be It! Act It!
An Alphabet of Positive Emotions and Feelings

https://corbettshwom.com

www.ingramcontent.com/pod-product-compliance
Lightning Source LLC
Chambersburg PA
CBHW041549040426
42447CB00002B/113

9 780578 335223